Dreams, Wishes and Fantasies of Common Folk

As Revealed in Old Photos, Folk Poetry and Art

B.G. Webb

authorHOUSE®

AuthorHouse™
1663 Liberty Drive
Bloomington, IN 47403
www.authorhouse.com
Phone: 1 (800) 839-8640

Published by AuthorHouse 12/24/2016

ISBN: 978-1-5246-5176-3 (sc)
ISBN: 978-1-5246-5175-6 (e)

Library of Congress Control Number: 2016919545

Print information available on the last page.

Any people depicted in stock imagery provided by Thinkstock are models,
and such images are being used for illustrative purposes only.
Certain stock imagery © Thinkstock.

This book is printed on acid-free paper.

Because of the dynamic nature of the Internet, any web addresses or links contained in
this book may have changed since publication and may no longer be valid. The views
expressed in this work are solely those of the author and do not necessarily reflect the
views of the publisher, and the publisher hereby disclaims any responsibility for them.

DEDICATION

TO
PRINCE, JUDY GARLAND AND ELVIS
PRESLEY WHOSE LIVES, MUSIC AND
UNIQUE SOUNDS AND PERFORMANCES
REFLECT THE DREAMING, WISHING
AND FANTASIZING OF COMMON FOLK

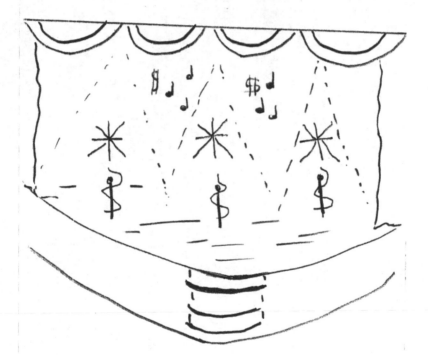

INTRODUCTION

This is a creative work that uses folk poems, old photos and art to probe into the minds of common folk as they reach for the stars to gain happiness and often get lost in the clouds.

As humans (and pets too) we must face the stress and emotional turmoil of the ups and downs of an ever-changing world. Many find the task unbearable and escape into the clouds as they try to reach the stars of everlasting happiness.

Some seek escape by wishing they were back at some happier time or place -- surrounded by people who love them.

Others live in a dream world. They fall asleep and find themselves in a more friendly world.

A few have horrible dreams -- nightmares -- that often result from the mind recalling frightening events that happened to them years ago.

Many seek refuge in a cloudy fantasy world. Indeed, they become different people -- not only in their dreams but in their everyday life. They often seek the care of mental professionals due to becoming victims of schizophrenia. Many do not seek professional medical help because being someone else makes them feel special -- gives them the attention that they need and love.

All these escapes into the clouds are ways that the minds of common folk survive. Without them there would be more suicides and or violent crimes against others.

Our journey into the workings of the mind will begin by viewing old black and white photos of people (and their pets) as they are seen in the light of everyday life. We will use our imaginations to speculate about what might happen to them mentally to wish, dream, have nightmares or fantasize that they are someone else or somewhere else.

When it comes to dreams, one can expect anything -- from getting an Oscar, becoming a Queen, dating a gorgeous woman to enjoying sexual desires that most consider "forbidden."

Then, you will read many folk poems about real people and pets who in order to cope have escaped into the clouds by wishing, dreaming or fantasizing that they are elsewhere or some other person.

One folk poem is about me. For years, I was under the care of a psychologist due to a recurring nightmare that resulted in seizures and screams.

Finally, you will find sketches of people and animals who are saying something that indicates that they are lost in the clouds of a wish, dream or fantasy.

At the conclusion, I will offer some reasons why so many use wishing, dreaming and fantasizing to get into the protective clouds as they reach for the stars of happiness.

I will offer some solutions to dealing with these human behaviors. All humans want happiness -- continual happiness. I feel that some of my suggestions for change might result in fewer people getting lost in the clouds and instead reach that star of happiness.

I have dedicated the book to three great performing artists whose lives symbolize the mental traumas that so many common folk experience in their lives. They are PRINCE, ELVIS PRESLEY AND JUDY GARLAND.

TABLE OF CONTENTS

FOLK POEMS

PHOTOS OF LIFE

Love

"Where will our love take us?"

Marriage

"We become one, but will it always be that way?"

Children

*"Well mom and dad, how
will you shape me?"*

Family

"Will the relationships within
the family be positive?"

Tucson   Sept. 1940

Pets

"Treat us nice and we will love you unconditionally."

Objects of Status

"Look what we have!"

In-Groups

"We want to be part of the gang!"

Outsiders

"We want to fit in and be accepted."

The EGO

"I'm so special!"

Pretending

"Look at us, we are ready for show biz."

FOLK POEMS

ODE TO PRINCE

Oh Prince -- you look like something from outer space
        when you come on stage to perform -- it's like you have
        decended from an UFO.

Why? Because of

      --- the glitter

      --- the lights

      --- the sparkling costumes

      --- the beat and rythum of the music.

You're so small -- and yet have a
        magnetic power that draws us to you.

You sing songs of the life of a
        pop star - a rap star -- of young people seaching for love--
        happiness -- a need of belonging.

What are my favorite songs that you zap out?

      "Let's Go Crazy"

      "Kiss"

      "I wanna Be Your Lover"

      "Partyman"

      "U Got the Look"

Oh Prince -- how I wish to hug you -- kiss you
      as we unite together in your sound -- your beat --
      your rap words of love.

Prince -- You are truly the king of pop, rap and zap.

Ode To Judy Garland

Judy -- sweet Judy!
How I adore you and your
unique sound.

When you sing, you capture the
emotions -- the tenderness of our feelings --

of our yearning for happiness -- our dreams.

-- yes even our fantasies.

And your eyes Judy do the same things--

they see our feelings, our longings, our dreams
-- and yes even our fantasies.

What are my favorite songs that you sing?

"Over the Rainbow"

"I Got Ghythm"

"Have Yourself A Merry Little Christmas"

"Swanee"

"Meet Me in St. Louis"

Oh Judy, we love you --
we want to hug you, kiss you and
hold you close.

B.G. WEBB

As you sing songs of our longings, our dreams, our
wishes, we want to protect you so we can always
hear your unique voice and feel the tenderness of
your sound.

Oh Judy, you are the Queen of All Hearts!
We will always remember you dancing
and singing down that yellow brick road
and being on stage with Mickey Rooney
in Babes on Broadway.
In so many of your performances you
sang about dreams, wishes and fantasies
of what life should be -- a JOY!

Ode to Elvis Presley

Oh Elvis baby,
    You light up the world with
your music -- that Rock and Roll sound.

When you come on stage something
    magic happens -- Why?
Here's why:

    your gorgeous face,

    your glittering costumes,

    your swinging hips and butt,

    Your sparkling - diamond studded belts
        around that slim waist.,

    your voice that echoes out
        dreams,

    wishes

    fantasies
-- and our forbidden sexual desires.

Oh Baby, you were unforgettable as you
    performed your classics:

    "Heartbreak Hotel"

    "Love Me Tender"

"Can't Help Falling in Love"

"Jailhouse Rock"

Oh Elvis,

Wish you would come down from wherever
you are and give us, if only
for one perforance, a chance to

Dream again

Wish Again

Fantasize again

That We are On That Stage With You and that You Smile and Say
"I love you baby."

The Lady who flew the British flag

We had a lady
        living in our neighborhood
by the name of
        Mrs. Chase.

She lived in a
        beautiful brick
mansion that was
        set in a large
park-like setting.

She was the widow of
        Gerald Chase
who had been one of
        the big shots at
Deere and Company.

She was well traveled,
        in fact, she had
taken the Graf Zipplin
        to Europe and returned
on the Queen Mary.

She had plenty of
        dough because she
had maids, cooks, a butler
        and a
Chauffeur to drive her in
        her Lincoln Limo.

We hardly ever saw
        her except when she was
driven to Davenport to
        do some shopping
at the best shops in
        our metro area.

Often she would be
        driven to the train
station to meet guests
        arriving on the
Golden State Limited.

Often we would see her
        guests enjoy
luncheon on the estate
        grounds and be
entertained by a small
        orchestra.

Then, one day we noticed
        something new.
What you ask? Well, at 7:00AM.
        the butler would
come out and raise the Union Jack
        on the flag pole.

We all wondered what
        was going on.
Did the old girl think
        she was living in
England?

One of the cooks said
        that Mrs. Chase now
always wanted to include
        time for tea.

And, get this, she
        insisted that the tea
be brewed in the English
        manner -- no tea bags.

It was reported that one
        day she called in
all the staff and told them
        that they should
refer to her as "Lady Chase."

When she entertained
        guests and served tea
she would serve cucumber
        sandwiches and
biscuits. They were what we
        would call cookies
but she insisted that the
        British word "biscuit"
be used.

Well, you can imagine our surprise
        when one day she sold
her Lincoln Limo and bought
        a Rolls-Royce.

Then, one day it was confirmed
        that the old girl
had lost it --- believed that
        she was living in England
and was of noble birth.

How you ask? Well, she was
        being driven in her
Rolls and she looked out the
        window and waved at us
in a royal manner -- she used
        her hand to wave in a
circular manner.
        Yes, we all knew that
she must have thought that she
        was Queen Mary.

The boy who dreams of flaming torches and breaking glass.

The dream always begins the same
      -- the flaming torches and
then the sounds of:
      running on the pavement,

      fists pounding on doors,

      glass breaking,

      then screams and cries for help.

In the dream I find myself
      looking out of a window.
I see flaming torches go by.
      Then streams of blood
flow down the window.

When I look through the glass,
      I see eyes -- lifeless --
dead eyes on faces that have
      been cut with knives.

In the dream I am helped by
      dark figures who seem
scared and frightened.

I am bundled up and
      carried to a waiting car.
After a long drive I am
      handed over to others.

Yes, I remember another thing --
        someone kissing me tenderly
on the forehead and my cheeks and
        then whispering,
"Auf Wiedersehen mein liebes Kind."

I have had this nightmare
        many times and I have
sought professional help. Why?
        Because of my fear of

        flaming torches,

        breaking glass,

        loud noises,

        pounding.

The sight and hearing the above
        cause me to have seizures.

I shake, scream and
        fall to the floor or pavement.

The nightmare continues to
        this day.

I see and hear all of these
        frighting things and sounds.

Always, at the end of the horror
        is the whispering of
"Auf Wiedersehen mein liebes Kind."

The dog who thought he was the coach
of the St. Louis Cardinals.

Dakota was his name
      and he thought he was
the coach of the St. Louis
      Cardinals.

How did he get that
      illusion you ask?
Well, he owed it all to
      his owner whose
name was Dorthea.

Yes, Dorthea first made
      Dakota into a fan
and then his ego took
      over after that and
he thought he was the
      coach of the team.

It didn't take Dorthea
      long to transform
Dakota into not only a fan
      but a coach as well.

You see, dear reader, he had
      all the fine qualities
that a Golden Retriver is
      known for:

B.G. Webb

intelligence,
confidence,
trustworthiness,
kindness,
and
friendliness.

And, besides that he was like
      Dorthea -- had redish brown
hair -- appeared as alert as a
      red cardinal in spring.

Yes, Dorthea would hold
      Dakota close to her
in front of the TV during
      game time and then
before each inning sing:

"Take me out to the ball game,
Take me out to the crowd,
buy me some peanuts and
      crackerjacks,
I don't care if I never
      get back."

During the song,
      Dakota would smile
and howl with his deep voice
      at the end of each
joyful stanza.

Then, he would be
        rewarded with crackerjacks
from a bag that Dorthea
        had been enjoying.

Of course, she bought a
        Cardinal cap and
an XXL Cardinal shirt
        for Dakota to wear
for each game and around
        the neighborhood.

When a Cardinal player
        hit a home run,
Dakota would smile and
        howl with delight.
Of course, Dorthea would
        give him a big hug and
lots of crackerjacks.

However, if a player
        would strike out,
or be sent to the dug out,
        Dakota would bark
and jumped up and down.

Yes, Dakota was well known
        in his part of town
for being a Cardinal fan and
        coach, with a keen instinct
for predicting the outcomes
        of games and who was
going to the World Series.

When Dorthea took him
        around the neighborhood
dressed in his Cardinal cap and
        shirt, neighbors would
ask, "Well, tell us Dakota,
        whose going to win
this Saturday?"

And Dakota would tell them.
        If he barked a lot and wagged
his tail, it meant a Cardinal win.
        If he lowered his head and put his
tail between his legs, then it meant
        a defeat for the Cardinals.

You may not believe this,
        but Dakota was right all of the time.
Yes, he was a brave and loyal Cardinal fan
        who had the keen instinct for the game
that would rival King Solomon at bat.

The lady who always wore black.

Caroline was her
        name and she
always wore back
        where ever she went --
        stores,
        churches
        weddings
        visits
        etc.

She was a teller
        at the U.S. Bank
before and after
        her marriage to
Patrick. She wore brightly
        colored outfits
that were beautifully
        coordinated
with shoes, purses, scarfs
        and everything else.

She was a beauty
        with her lush black hair,
blue eyes and gorgeous
        figure that were
a match to her smile that
        seemed to light up
every gathering that she
        attended.

How did she come to wear
        black you ask?
It was the war -- it changed
        everything.
You see Patrick was killed
        during the Battle of the
Bulge and Caroline lost
        what gave her that
radiant smile.

Caroline never got over it
        -- the telegram that he was
missing -- and another
that he had been killed.

After that -- the return of the
        body -- or what was left of it --
and the burial in the military
        cemetery at the Rock Island
Arsenal.

She dressed in black
        for the funeral --
black veil and gloves --
        everything in black.
She literally became a
        shadow in black.

She stood by the grave
        as taps were played
and rifles fired.
        When it started to
rain, she found herself enclosed
        in black umbrellas
raised by kind souls who wished
        to protect and hug her.

Afterward she found herself
        locked in black --
locked in morning for Patrick.
        Infact, she found
comfort in the darkness --
it enclosed her and in some
        strange way brought
her comfort.

You see, dear reader, she and
        Patrick were a perfect match.
When they said "I do" their
        souls were forever united.

The phrase "until death" didn't apply
        to their special relationsiip --
they were eternally united.
        At their wedding they truly
became one spiritually.

Some criticized her for
        morning so long --
for not getting over it
        -- that wearing black
        made others depressed.

Caroline turned a deaf ear
        to those remarks and
continued to wear black
        for the rest of her
life.

Why you ask?
        It was the only way that
she could cope with the
        terrible loss of the
love of her life.

Much later, when she was
        dying at a nursing home,
she told her kinfolk, "Dress me
        in my wedding dress when
I'm in the casket. I want to
        to surprise Patrick
when I see him in Heaven."

Dreaming of a Menage a Trois

I went to sleep
    and dreamed
I went to
    a massage parlor
and fell in love
    with two Sweds.

When I went in
    for the treatment,
I had no idea that
    I would become
deeply involved with
    what they call
A MENAGE A TROIS.
    But I did and
it was wonderful.

The parlor was
    opperated by
Brunhilda and Kunther
    Swanson.

At first I thought
    they were a married
couple and then
    found out they were
brother and sister.

Both were trim and
    muscular, blonde --with
blue eyes and bright
    welcoming smiles.

I had some difficulty
        understanding their
accent but soon adjusted and
        found their English
cute and charming.

When I started going
        I had Kunther for my
treatments.

I would strip
        and lay on a table
that had a soft blue pad
        on it.

Kunther would start
        the treatments with
hot towels to relax the
        muscles and open up
the pores of my skin.

After that he would
        gently remove the
towels and use his hands
        to massage:

        neck
        shoulders
        chest
        waist
        buttocks
        thighs
        legs
        feet.

He must have had a foot fetish
        because when he got
to my feet, he would gently
        suck and kiss
each toe.

After he finished the
        back side,
he would gently turn
        me on my back and
work on the front side
        of the body.

During the treatment
        he would ask again and again,
"Does that feel good?"
        I always said, "Ah yes!"

When he got to your cock
        and balls, he would
use a small hot towel to
        twirl them around
a bit.

Then, he would ask, "Does that
        relax your manhood?"
I always replied, "Ah yes, it
        feels wonderful."

He was very happy to hear that
        and said that I had
experienced his own maneuver
        which he invented.
He called it the "Kunther Twril."

During each treatment,
   he enjoyed chatting with me
He asked about my occupation, interests,
   and marriage status.

At the end of the session,
   he always brought in the
hot bamboo sticks for
gently beating the back and
   the buttocks.

Then, one day I found the
   his sister Brunhilda
was going to do the treatment.
   She went through the
same step by step therapy
   with gentle skill.

I have to admit that when she
   did do the "Kunther Twril"
I got a heart on my cock. But
   she just smiled and
commented, "Oh what a compliment!"

I finally asked her but for a
   date and we wound up at
her place in her bedroom making
   passionate love.

Wow, making love to her was
   fantastic. She had
a vagina, with muscles that
   could tighten or
expand to give your cock
   a glorious feel.

This went on for months. Then,
        once Kunther appeared.
Yes, he opened the bedroom door
        and smiled as he saw me
humping his sister.

He said, softly, "May I join in
        with the fun?"
Without a hesitation, we both
        said, "Sure, welcome aboard."
I guess that we were in such a
        state of bliss that we
wanted to share the experience
        Besides, Kunther was kinfolk
and a pal.

He took off his clothes,
        grabed a Trojan rubber and
the tube of K-Y and slip his dick
        up my ass. Then we began
rocking back and forth. Wow! He
        hit my G-spot again and
again.
        After we came,
we all laid together for a
        smile and a "joint" and
enjoyed that post-fuck feeling
        of tranquility.

WAKE UP

"What happened? Cum is all
over me. Must have had a
wet dream.
        Wow! I feel great."

The man who was only seen at night.

I was told
      that his name was Fred,
the son of the custodian
      at Willard Grade School.

Nobody ever saw him
      except at night
when he would leave his
      parent's home and walk
around the town.

No one ever talked
      about him.
His life's story was
      covered in darkness
and told in whispers.

I only found out more
      about him as a result
of running into him one night
      and then asking Caroline,
our next door neighbor
      about him.

It must have been
      9:00 P.M. when the "Night Man"
(that is what the kids called him)
      practically collided with me
along the tree lined street.

I remember hearing his
        steps in the Autumn leaves
and then seeing the silhouette
        of a tall figure coming
suddenly toward me.

He had a cap on
        and wore a black trench coat
and I called out "Hello!"
        He responded with silence --
he simply glided by me.

Later, I would be told by
        Caroline that he had been born
to the Smiths in the 1920's
        and was mentally retarded
and hence remained at home.

I often wondered
        what he did all day long
in his 2nd floor room in
        the frame house that
the Smith's owned on 12th Ave.

I never found out.
        The "Night Man" continued
to be seen by a few -- walking
        in the darkness -- forever
lost in his dream world.
        Perhaps, the only sounds he
ever heard were the rustling of
        Autumn leaves and the
hooting of owls.

The dog who took Miss Isabella for a stroll.

Miss Isabella was a
        lady in my neighborhood
who lived in her own
        dream world.

Her only friend and
        companion was her
Siberian husky, whose
        name was Chipper.

She was the only daughter of
        the Deere family
that had established the
        now famous John Deere Co.

The family lived in a
        beautiful Victorian mansion
overlooking a vast wooded estate
        which was filled with
small bridges over streams and
        statues of Greek gods.

Isabella was a lovely child
        with hair the color of
strawberries and blue eyes that
        reminded one of the
Mediteranean Sea.

B.G. Webb

She was kept away from other
        children and waited on
by nannies and maids.
        She was treated as if she
were a princess of the House of
        Windsor.

After graduating from an
        exclusive private school,
she had been sent off to a
        finishing school in
England.

There, she met her first
        Silberian husky.
He was the school's
        mascot and his
name was Chipper.

Well, she fell in love
        with him.
He was so handsome with
        his white fur
and noble bearing. He had
        all the qualities
of his breed:

        intelligence,

        gentleness,

        friendliness and

        keen alertness.

When Isabella returned,
        she had a social
"coming out" party
        along with other
debutantes.

While she had many
        gentlemen callers,
none were considered
        worthy of her --
or at least that's what
        her parents thought.

So, she never married
        and stayed home
and spent her time doing
        needlepoint,
crocheting and in the spring
        and summer
gardening.

One thing that brighted up
        her days was her
pet dog --- and the dog that
        she selected was
always a husky and was always
        named Chipper.

The neighbors got used to
        seeing the two together
-- walking or tending to the
        garden -- especially
the pink and red roses.

When they were seen taking a
          stroll, it was a quite a
beautiful sight. Isabella always
          wore something elegant
and colorful -- and of course very
          stylish to match her own
beauty and pose.

As she got into her 70's,
          she seemed to be losing it.
Yes, it now looked as if Chipper
          was taking Miss Isabella
out for a stroll rather than
          the other way around.

Chipper always walked
          with great confidence
and with a wide smile
          on his handsome face.

You could tell
          that he felt in charge.
How you ask?
          Well, his tail was always
up and his walk was that of a
          horse at Buckingham Palace.

Yes, they made quite a pair.
          -- so involved in their
stroll but you could tell that
          they were bonded together
in trust, in their togetherness and
          may I be bold enough to say,
in their love for each other.

The lovely and innocent girl who became a high-priced whore in Chicago.

On Classmates.com
      they are always asking,
"Does anyone know where Sherri Newman is?"
      Well, I know -- in Chicago
operating a whore house for
      high priced clients. Now she
calls herself Miss Rita Devine.

      At one time she was known
      in Chicago as one "hot mama."

You ask, "How did that happen?"
      Here's Sherri's or Rita's story.

When I met her in junior high,
      she was a lovely and innocent
girl -- as sweet as apple pie.

She had auburn hair, blue eyes
      and a lovely smile
that often was the start of a
      gentle laugh that
could bring joy to any group.

I remember she was so polite --
      always listening to my concerns
-- so caring and concerned.

She lived with her father
	who was a widower.
He was an attractive, good
	natured guy who worked hard at his
cafeteria which served good food
	for reasonable prices.

So, what went wrong you ask?
	Well she started dating
Hank Crawford.
	He was a possessive son of a bitch
-- only out to satisfy his
	horny desires.

Sherri got pregant
	and Hank abondoned her.
Sherri had the baby and then
	it was adopted out.

At that point in her life,
	everyone -- including her father --
seemed to blame her and avoided her.
	She was "the town's whore."

After the birth of the baby
	and his adoption,
Sherri was in despair and she
	felt that the only reason
guys liked her was for sex.

She often could be seen in
        cars with a lot of guys
during lunch hour -- driving
        around and letting them
have all the loving they wanted.

After she father died, she
        inherited a lot of money.
She decided to take the dough and
        make herself over and move to
Chicago to become a high priced hooker.

Yes, she went to the best
        beauty shops in town and
had herself made over -- blonde hair,
        red nail polish, facial make up
to suit a STAR.

Yes, she wanted that -- become
        a STAR in the whore game.
She spent money on her clothes too
        and purchased a lot of
high heel shoes.

She also learned all the dances
        -- waltz, tango, rumba,
etc. so she could give the guys
        a good time.

Off to Chicago she went.
        Found a pimp to round up
clients and she made plenty of money
        and became Rita -- "the hot mama"
from Chicago.

Later she opened up her own
        house of pleasure on the
North Side where all the money was
        and hired gorgeous gals who
knew how to give guys a great time
        in the bedroom.

Yes, in her mind Sherri or Rita had
        become a STAR.
She lived in a fantasy world of her own
        making.

I have never informed Classmates.com
        about where Sherri is because to me
her story is a sad one -- one that reminds
        us all that not all find a kind
stranger when they need one and deserve
        help.

DREAMING ABOUT BEING ON
TOP OF THE SANDPILE

I sit here high on top of a lofty sandpile with my dog Peggy,
  feeling the warm sand underneath,
and looking at the Mississippi River.
  It's my favorite place in all the world.

It's located off 1st Avenue
  near factories and foundries,
In fact, the sand is here to be used
  by the workers in the plants.

I love to be way up here
  and look down at Dad and others fishing along the wharf.
On my right I see the suspension bridge to Bettendorf,
  and on my left several barges coming down the river.

There, way off in the distance, I can make out
  three speed boats churning up the muddy waters.
In back of me are railroad tracks that are used by
  the Rock Island Lines.

Far across to the other side of the river,
  I can see more factories, oil tanks, water towers
  and moving cars and trucks.
The fumes from smoke stacks and locomotives mingle with
  the smell of the river.

I marvel at the size of the river,
  and its powerful current.
It is a force of nature that provides so much
  and yet must be distrusted for its untamed ways.

Peggy and I only come down from our lofty perch
        to eat with the family, throw stones into the river
and run along the beach,
        chasing dragonflies.

As night falls, the lights along the river banks are
        reflected in the water.
Then fireflies appear to play games along with other
        critters in the moon light.

Before my family leaves, Dad gathers up the fish he caught
        while Mom fills up the picnic basket with dirty dishes.
Sometimes I bag or box up some of the sand for my
        sandbox at home.

As we leave I always find myself looking forward to coming again
        to the river bank --- to once again climb to the
top of the sandpile so that I can feel the warmth of the sand
        and enjoy the view of life along the river.

DREAMING I'M WALKING DOWN THE ALLEYS

What will I discover on this warm June day as I walk down the alleys
between 11th and 12th Avenues?

As usual I see plenty of trash cans and, oh yes, the hollyhocks. My, aren't
they pretty --- with their bright reds, pinks and purples.

Let's see, Mrs. Patterson and Miss Johnson are hanging out their wash.

Hey! What's that on the line? A new type of girdle? I guess so.

And, I declare, Mrs. Patterson has some new panties --- light purple no less.

What is that? Burning trash. And nobody is around to watch it. Well, I'm
sure Mr. Applegate will hear from his neighbors --- especially the ones
hanging out their clothes to dry. Yuck! Smells like burning rubber.

Watch out! Bobby Bell and his gang are playing kickball. Looks like fun but
that ball could go anywhere.

And there is John and Paul Koster playing basketball --- with great skill
too. That-away guys!

Oh, some of the garage doors are open. There's Mr. Patterson waxing his
Buick and over there is Mr. Frunk trying to start his Hudson. Not
having much luck either.

There goes little Lennie Johnson with his red wagon filled with dirt, sand
and rocks. I wonder what he is up to.

In the Smith's backyard I see their little girls playing in their round tin
wading pool. And, not far away their older brothers have invited some
friends to play volleyball.

Hey, up in the sky I see a kite --- looks like the American flag. Oh, now I
see who's flying it --- Buddy Webb. Boy, he is an odd one. Likes to do
things by himself.

There is Kelly Benson out in his Victory Garden --- doing some hoeing. I
yell, "How are your tomatoes coming along?" Kelly replies, "Coming ---
coming along."

Wow! What an eye full. That Lisa Turner is really something in a bathing
suit. Out sunning herself again. I can see why she is so popular with
the men. And, she has some money too what with working at the
defense plant at the Rock Island Arsenal.

Watch out! Here comes George Wood in his '39 Buick. At 78 he can hardly navigate that long thing. He should stop driving. He can hardly see anymore. Lord, he might hit a child someday. He's a good old soul --- always waves and smiles as he passes by but someday he could hit somebody.

Well, I'm nearing the end of the alley. Got to get back. My, do I have a lot to tell the folks.

Nothing like going down an alley to get some news.

WISHING I WAS BACK IN THE WOODS

The woods along 11th Avenue in my neighborhood are lush and deep.

They hold many secrets within their dark ravines and pathways.

Most are only known by the children who are brave enough to explore them.

The adults are too busy making money and doing chores to venture into a tameless natural world.

Most consider going into the woods is a waste of time --- and a childish thing to do.

Some men in the neighborhood on rare occasions go into the woods because they know one secret that they can use --- the best fishing worms can be found by digging at the bottom of the ravines.

You have to talk to the children to find out all the really important secrets of the woods.

They will tell you that there are secret pathways that are good short-cuts to 19th Street.

All will tell you about the small clear stream that flows from 17th Street to 19th Street --- and the bridge that spans it.

They love to tell about finding it --- going along a narrow path near the stream until in the brush up ahead one spots in the distance the concrete bridge.

They will also tell you that magnolia trees are planted on both sides of the curved bridge --- and that in the spring, their large pink blooms create a fairy-like world.

Built by the Good family whose estate is located high on the bluff overlooking the stream, it was to be enjoyed by fine ladies and gentlemen who wanted to enjoy the beauties of the natural world. Of course, it has now been long forgotten.

The children also know that the woods are filled with flowers. Violets, buttercups and wild roses can be picked in the spring for May baskets.

They also know that gangs of kids have created battle camps in the woods so that they can play war games. They all pretend that they are attacking Germans or Japanese soldiers.

Some of the children also know another secret --- that one way to feel the presence of God is by being part of the natural world.

As they stand still along a path and look up at the blue sky through the lush foliage and listen to the sounds of birds and other creatures, they sense the oneness of all living things.

A few of the children in winter go into the snow-covered woods to build secret hide-aways. As they sit quietly in their self-made winter camps and hear the wind rustling though the tree branches, they sense how small they are in the great scheme of things.

Too bad more adults can't take the time to explore the woods and rediscover their bond of kinship with nature.

The Secret Bridge

WISHING I WAS BACK AT WILLARD GRADE SCHOOL

Oh how I would love to go back to Willard --- that old rust-colored brick school where as a child I learned, explored and played.

I can picture it in my mind's eye --- two stories, fire escapes, a tall smoke stack, playgrounds and the flagpole displaying Old Glory.

In back was the storage place for coal which was kept filled all winter long by Mr. Smith, the janitor.

He was a tall, white-haired and kindly man who enjoyed talking to us children.

Even now I can hear the echoes made by the steps of students as they passed the bust of Emma Willard and made their way up and down the wooden corridors and steep staircases.

I can feel the excitement and joy of being dismissed for recess. The girls would play hopscotch and jumping rope while the boys turned to kickball and marbles.

I can picture the long narrow cloakrooms and smell the damp clothes hung there during wet and snowy weather.

And, in December I joined others in being in awe of the huge Christmas tree that was put up in the main hall --- with its bright lights, gleaming ornaments and fresh pine smell.

I can also see all those caring teachers:

Miss Long helping us build a model of a B-29 bomber and letting us name it "The Merry Christmas";

Miss Hansen asking us to bow our heads in a silent prayer on D-Day;

Miss Swanson with her ever-present pitchpipe leading us in song and telling us "to sing out" and "stay on key";

Miss Benson helping us organize a Valentine party and making sure everyone received cards;

Miss Peterson, our principal, telling us Patrol Boys to be "ever so watchful" as we did our duty;

and, Miss Hill helping us practice doing the Maypole dance so we could present it at Wharton Field House.

I remember that May was always such a special month because that's when the school raised money by having a carnival.

Since it was a night event, I recall how I felt that the old school was transformed into a fairyland with food stands, a movie theater and booths that offered games of chance.

Our parents helped out by baking goodies and manning the booths. My mom loved to help out at the "fishing pond."

In the auditorium students performed acts. There was always a Fred Astaire and a Ginger Rogers doing a dance number and a Houdini doing a magic act.

Oh, how I would love to go back for a day to visit old Willard in order to enjoy the atmosphere, see all my school chums and especially say "thank you" to all those caring teachers.

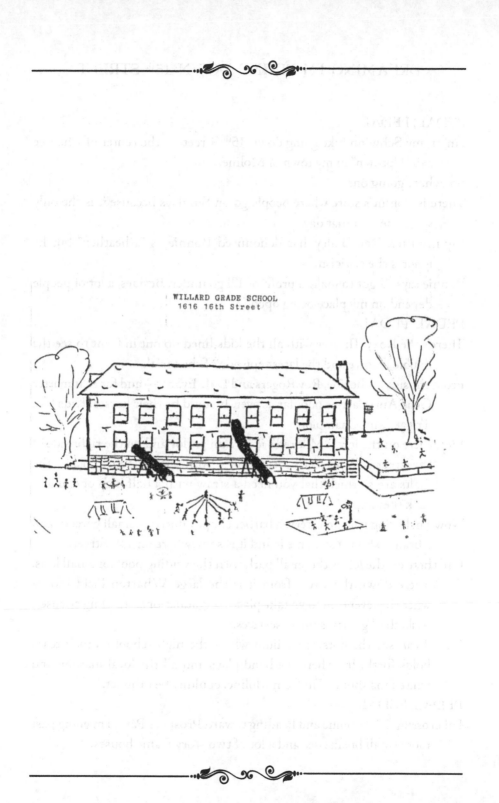

WILLARD GRADE SCHOOL
1616 16th Street

DREAMING I'M BIKING DOWN 15th STREET

PEDAL, PEDAL

I'm on my Schwinn bike going down 15th Street --- the center of what we call "Uptown" in my town of Moline.

So, what's going on?

There is Bonnie's store where people go on Sundays because it is the only store open on that day.

My minister, Rev. Bailey, has denounced Bonnie as "a heathen" but he ignores the criticism.

Bonnie says, "I got to make a profit or I'll go under. Besides, a lot of people depend on my place being open."

PEDAL, PEDAL

There's the Roxy Theater with all the kids lined up out in front to see the double feature and the latest episode of the serial.

From the size of the line, Roy Rogers and Dale Evans --- and for that matter Gene Autry are as popular as ever. It could be their horses. Kids love Trigger and Champion.

Hey, there on the left is Mildred's ice cream parlor and on the right side of the street is Wheelock's Drug Store. Both serve good ice cream. The malts are so thick that you need a straw with a half-inch opening to suck them up.

Now I'm biking past an eatery, a barber shop, a florist, a small gorcery and a beauty shop. You name it and it is somewhere on 15th Street.

Oh, there on the left is the small park with the wading pool for small kids.

And, there down the street from it is the large Wharton Field House where big events in town take place --- graduations, traveling circuses, basketball games, sunrise services.

Now I can see the outside stadium where the high school football team holds forth. It's where the band plays and all the loyal maroon and white fans shout: "I'm from Moline, couldn't be prouder."

PEDAL, PEDAL

I'm crossing 23rd Avenue and heading toward Prospect Park. I'm going past more small businesses and a lot of two story frame houses.

I'm turning into the park and going down the winding road that circles the pond. I see a few men fishing.

Hey, there are the ducks. Some kids are feeding them and a few have actually gotten out of the water to take some of the "handouts."

Oh, what's over there --- a young couple making whoopee on a blanket? I think the guy has his hands up her skirt. I'm going back for a second look.

PEDAL, PEDAL

The guy saw me staring. Oh no, he is getting up. He's going to run after me. Better beat it fast.

Wow! I made it. I'm out of the park. Boy, have I seen a lot today. Can't wait to tell the guys about the lovers.

You sure can learn a lot by going down 15th street.

DREAMING ABOUT STEPHENS SQUARE

Where am I? Oh, there's the Woolworth Store. And across the street is the First National Bank.

Hey, there's a street sign. I'm at the corner of 5th Avenue and 15th Street.

I know where I am. I'm at busy Stephens Square in the heart of Moline.

Look at all the old cars, trucks and busses. It must be old Moline --- sometime in the early 1950s.

My, so many shoppers. Everytime the traffic light changes, at least thirty people rush across the street.

Look at all the familiar stores. There's The New York Store on my left and across from it is Josephson Jewelers.

Oh look, there is their big clock out front.

Then down 15th Street are all the big stores --- Penneys, Montgomery Wards and Sears.

No wonder the place is so busy --- this was the center of business for many. A lot of people worked and shopped here.

What! I can't believe it. There's Miss Hendee. "Hi Miss Hendee! Boy you look good. Do you still teach American Literature at the High School?" She just nods and smiles.

Who is that over there. Why it's Mr. Bean, my old geometry teacher. "How are you doing?" He waves and smiles at me.

That's another thing about the square. You could meet just about everyone in town sometime at the square. Just about everyone came here to bank, to shop, to eat and just to see what was going on.

This was the place where all the big events of the town took place too.

I remember coming here to see the big parade celebrating V-E Day and later V-J Day.

This was the place the high school band came as part of Homecoming. And the pep rally was held here too.

Some of the big events celebrating Moline's centennial in 1948 were held right here in Stephens Square.

What a place! It brought people together. It gave them excitement. It was the center of community life.

And oh, at Christmas, this was the place to be --- street lamps with all their decorations and the stores all done up in red and green. That New York Store was one of the best what with laurels with lights cascading down the front of the building to the street.

I awaken with a smile. I say to myself, "It was great going back to that square. I wonder if the square is still the center of things. I hope so. Every town needs a square like Stephens Square to give it a sense of excitement, community and pride."

Then I thought, "Hell, anytime I'm blue I'm going to take a nap and dream about the square. It sure gave me a lot of happy memories."

WISHING TO BE BACK AT MY OLD HIGH SCHOOL

It remains in my mind as a beacon of hope --- a shining city on a hill, a source of pride.

In pep assemblies before games, I would shout: "I'm from Moline, couldn't be prouder --- if you can't hear me, I'll yell it a little louder."

The school had lots of character with its medieval towers, arches and gable roofs.

Inside along the main corridor were plaster reliefs of scenes from Greek and Roman epics.

A tall statue of Athena and another of Artemis stood guard on either side of the stage in the auditorium.

The school offered opportunities for students to learn, to express themselves, to compete, to explore, to excel.

Its fine teachers knew their subjects, possessed enthusiasm for learning and had the skills to reach a variety of students.

In my memory I can see myself back there performing in a Shakespearean play, dribbling a basketball down the court, giving a speech, doing an experiment in the lab, writing a theme, doing research at the library.

It offered a lot of fun too --- especially at the REK where you could dance and play ping pong.

It gave you something to look forward to --- like getting the latest issue of the <u>Line</u> <u>O'</u> <u>Type</u> or letting your pals sign their names in the <u>N</u> after it came out.

While the old school has been abandoned years ago, its legacy lives on in the minds of its graduates.

Its traditions have been transferred to the new high school for other generations.

Recently, when I returned to the old building and walked down its hallowed halls, I thought I heard coming from he the auditorium: "I'm from Moline, couldn't be prouder --- if you can't hear me, I'll yell it a little louder."

Could it be that the souls of many former students have returned to the place where they were truly happy?

Do they spend their days reading old copies of <u>The Imp</u>, <u>Line O' Type</u> and the "<u>M</u>"?

Do they still dance and play ping pong at the REK?

Have the souls of many teachers returned too? Has Miss Garst returned to direct another Shakespearean play?

Is Miss Hendee still holding forth about the works of Edgar Allan Poe?

Has Mr. Foley returned to coach basketball?

Does Mr. Swanson still help students perform experiments in the lab?

And, is it possible that Miss Becker is back directing the choir?

Has the outspoken and worldly Mr. Nuquist returned to sponsor the debate team?

Could it be that the grads plan a "swingout" and a prom at the end of the term?

Is the old school still a beacon of hope --- a shining city on the 16th Street hill? I'd like to think so.

Good Old M.H.S.

B.G. WEBB

The lady who wished for a burial plot and a grave stone.

Pat was her name
          and she did not
wish to be
          forgotten.

She knew that she
          would be part
of the family
          history.

Her children told her
          that she would be
remembered with love
          and tenderness.

It was the fact that
          she would not have a
burial plot that
          troubled her deeply.

You see her husband --and she
          did herself for a while --
felt that a plot wasn't necessary.
          One's soul went on to another
existence -- the body would be
          left behind.

They had agreed to will
          their bodies to science
and then the parts that were
          not used would be cremated.

But, now she felt that
      there should be a small part
of the earth where at least a
      memorial marker could be
placed with their names on it.

Such a marker would be there
      not only for future members of
the family, but for strangers who
      went by to read, if not to remember
them, but to at least know that such
      people existed for a time.

Yes, to be remembered
      was important to Pat.
Her name engraved on a marker
      would be proof that she had existed
in that form at one time.

TO BE REMEMBERED ----

    ISN'T THAT SOMETHING WE ALL WISH FOR?

The girl who dreamed she was accused of not being proud to be black and beautiful.

Oh no! I'm back in my
        American Problems class.
And I can't believe it --
        there is LaTasha who was
so mean to me.

And next to her is Larry --
        the president of the
Back Students for Awareness
        and Action.

Ooh I've got to wake up --
        this is a nightmare.

Oh my God, Latasha is looking
        at black guys who have been dating
white girls. She speaks:

"You Black men have been brainwashed
        by the white dominated society
to believe that Afrian women are not
        beautiful. You want white women --
especially those that have Nordic charactertiscs --
        I'm talking about the blonde, blue-eyed
creatures that dominate the world of advertising.
        Well, I'm here to tell you that
I'm an African woman and I'm Black and Beautiful."

Oh No! Now she is glaring at me.
 She shouts: "And, you. Anna, think
you're better than me because you have
 lovely straight hair and cream
colored skin -- you are accepted by
 many white students because
you look like one of them -- White and
 Beautiful.

Well, I going to tell you how you got
 that way --- Your grandma was raped by
a white slave owner -- yes that's that happened.
 And the result is that you are not
proud to be Black and Beautiful."

 ANNA WAKES UP IN A PANIC AND

THINKS: "Boy that LaTasha could scare the living shit out of you!"

The Persian Cat Who Thought She Was an Egyptian Queen

"I am a queen
      and yet my owners
--Jim and Sharen -- treat me
      like a common
household cat.

      Meow! Meow! Meow!

Can't they sense my
      royal bearing?
I'm all black except for
      my breast which is white.

      Meow! Meow! Meow!

My ears point upward
      to honor the sun.
When I sit, I am always
      like a queen sitting
in a glided chair
      on the dias of
a royal chamber.

      Meow! Meow! Meow!

Jim and Sharen are
      so reserved -- so
unto themselves --
      They have no time
to recognize and appreciate
      how my royal power
honors their household.

Meow! Meow! Meow!

They do not see that
        I'm descended from
the cats that served the
        great queens of Egypt:

Nefertiti

Cleopatra

Hatshepsut

        Meow! Meow! Meow!

Oh, I pray each day
        that they will get their minds
out of books and their eyes off of TV
        shows and DVDs
and awaken to see me for what
        I am -- a beautiful gift
from Egypt -- royal, wise, and
        majestic.

        Meow! Meow! Meow!

It would only take one
        long and insightful look
for them to observe how I
        honor that glorious
heavenly body --
        the Sun.

        Meow! Meow! Meow!

My black ears point up
        to praise that
glorious, heavenly body.
        My tail curls around my
still form and then points
        up to the Sun.

        Meow! Meow! Meow!

Yes, I even sing a hymn of praise
        to the Sun.

Meow! Meow!

        Oh God of Heaven.

Meow! Meow!
        How your bright rays give
                life to all.

Meow! Meow!

        How powerful is your life
                giving rays.

Meow! Meow!

        All stand to honor and to praise
                to the Sun.

Amen! Amen! Amen!

The horse who took Amanda everywhere.

She was known as
        Sally Anne
and she was the most
        gorgeous horse
in the valley.

She was born in a stable
        on a farm owned by
the Banister Family.

Like her mama and
        papa, she was a
beauty with her cream coat
        and white mane and tail.

Yes, she was descended
        from a long line of
beautiful Palominos
        and she was truly
gorgeous.

Amanda was only a
        child when she
met Sally Anne
        who was hitched
to the carriage that took
        the family to church.

When she got older,
	Amanda was taught
how to mount and use
	the reins to ride
Amanda around the open
	range that was part
of the Banister farm.

Yes, Sally Anne took
	Amanda and her folks
everywhere:
	to the store,
	to meetings,
	to auctions
	to the train station.

Amanda felt that
	she was Queen Victoria
everytime she rode in a carriage
	driven by her faithful and
trusted friend -- Miss Sally Anne.

Sally Anne was noted
	for her trod --
a moderately fast gait
	in which her legs
moved in diagonal pairs.

Yes, she trodded with
      elegance and grace.
Amanda felt that Sally Anne
      knew she was the
Queen's horse -- and Victoria's
      at that.

And, believe it or not,
      but Sally Anne felt that
she was driving the Queen of England
      whereever she wanted to go.

And, on the day Amanda was married,
      Sally Anne believed more than
ever that she was driving the Queen
      to the church to marry
her prince charming.

Oh yes, on the day "Here Comes the Bride"
      was played at the church, both

Amanda and Sally Anne knew
      who they were -- THE QUEEN AND HER
FAITHFUL HORSE.

The Latino who became the star stripper in all the "hot" L.A. Clubs.

Tony Costello was
        his name and
he danced and stripped
        at all the "hot"
clubs in Los Angeles.

Tony was the son of a
        drummer from Brazil
by the name of Francisco
        Costello.
So, he grew up hearing music.

His mother was a popular singer
        by the name of Delores Rio --
whose real name was Delores Smith
        from Cleveland, Ohio.

Francisco and Delores had met
        while performing in the
same night clubs in L.A. and
        fell passionately in love.

Well, their passion led to
        the birth of Anthony
who was called "Tony" by all.
        He inherited all their talents
-- a sense of rhythum, love of music
and a voice of a Elvis Presley.

Besides that he inherited all the
          good looks of his father --
tan skin, black eyes and
          a wonderful smile.

Oh, I should add that he was
          6'2" tall and had a
"package" that other boys
          envived because it
was long, thick and had a head
          the size of a golf ball.

Yes, indeed, Tony had it all
          -- looks, talent and well hung.
          When he was in P.E. playing
basketball, his manhood would
          often be seen seen dangling
          out of his jock strap
when he jumped up to make a basket.

When he turned 18, he decided
          to join his folks in Show Business.
He became a male stripper
          at the night clubs in L.A.

Why a stripper? Well he thought
          that would make him a star --
someone special. He tought, "With my
          looks and long cock,
and dancing ability, I would be a
          SENATION in capital letters."

As the band played "Runaway Train"
         he did his number.
He used two costumes -- a cowboy outfit
         for the gals and a Batman outfit
for the guys who went to gay bars.

As he danced on stage as a cowboy,
         he took off the following
and threw them to the audience:

         leather gloves

         leather vest

         leather pants

He was left with his mask, cowboy hat
         and G-string.

As he arched his butt toward the
         gals, they would slip bills
in his G-string.

For the guys he did the same
         routine and only left his
cowl on and black G-string.

Well, Tony was a sensation.
         By the way, he wasn't gay,
but a job is a job.
         The slogan in the biz. is:
"Accept a gig anywhere as long
         as you're paid."

As he became known for being "Mr. Big",
        he sometimes found notes with
phone numbers and big bills and offers to
        pay him more if he showed up to
lay the signer.

Well, Tony's view was: "If the offer is good
        and the gal/guy is hot, why not.
It's show business -- got to please my fans."

In his mind he was a STAR --
        SOMEONE SPECIAL
        A SENSATION.

The man who denied his wife was dead.

His name was Fred
        and when his wife died,
he fantasized that she
        was alive and well.

When you entered his home,
        the kitchen table was
set for two -- plates,
        silver ware and glasses --
even napkins.

His home was filled with photos
        of his beloved Louise.
All the photos were ones in which
she was cutting-up and cute --
        hugging their dog,
        making a funny face,
        dressed in one of her many
        costumes that she used
        to teach German and make her
        student enjoy each
                lesson.

Yes - there were photos showing her
        dressed as Brunnhilda
and, of course, the famous Cleopatra.
        Others showed her in costumes
for the holidays -- as a Bunny for
Easter, a pilgrim for Thanksgiving
        and as Mrs. Santa for
                Christmas.

When Fred got into his car,
      next to him were
things associated with Louise
      -- a Cubs Cap and a
shirt with Sammy Sosa's name on it.

When he sent cards to anyone,
      he always included her name.
He even enjoyed hearing her voice
      as he played a CD that she had
made when she interviewed her
      grandmother and talked about
her life back on the farm in Arkansas.

The sound of her voice and her
      laughter gave him so much
comfort. It was like she was there
      and enjoying going down
memory lane.

When anyone asked him
      how Louise was doing,
he said, "Oh, she is just fine --
      we all should be as happy
as she is."

ART

Sketches of People and Pets

"I wish I was sun bathing at a beach along the Mediteranean
Sea and being treated like an Italian film star."

B.G. WEBB

"I'm the greatest mind reader in the world."

"My strip act has made me a star."

B.G. WEBB

"Wow, I'm going to make love to her-- at least in my dreams."

"I'm related to the Vanderbilts you know."

B.G. Webb

"I'm the coach of the St. Louis Cardinals."

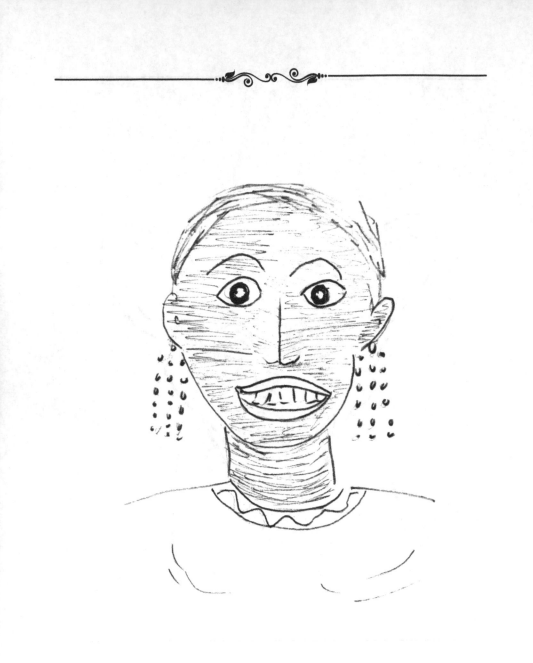

"I'm going to work for Opra. I got one of the leads in a film about a black family living during Reconstruction."

B.G. WEBB

"I wish I could remember my real name. I've had so many identities. Now, I can't remember who I was."

"Oh, I wish I was back on the Olympic fencing team in London. Boy, that was something. I felt special."

"I'm ready for the next shot. Being a porn star is great.
Can't wait for the guy to undress me and make love. I
see the camera crew is ready for my close-up."

"I'm the grandson of Hemingway, the great writer."

B.G. Webb

"You are wrong. My dear Ted is alive and well."

"I'm smiling because I remember playing Puck. Oh,
I'd love to go back to college again and be part of the
group that put on that play by Shakespeare.

"I wish my owners would give me more attention."

"I'm the reincarnation of Oscar Wilde."

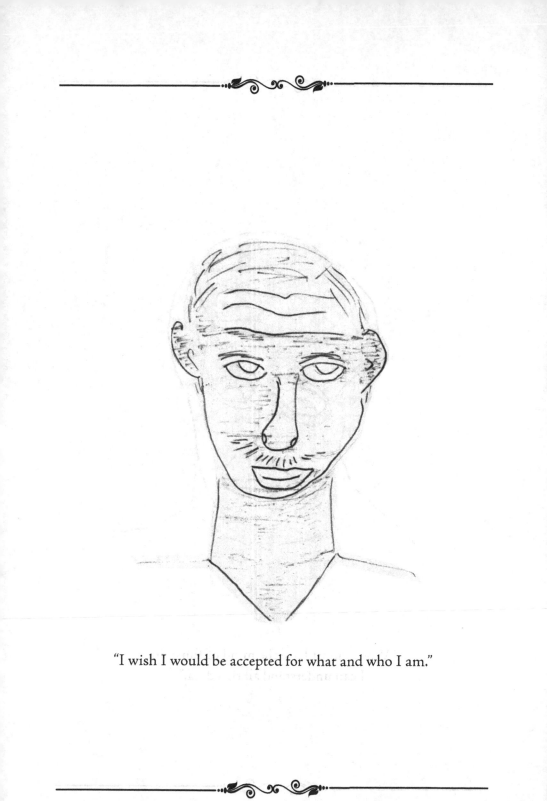

"I wish I would be accepted for what and who I am."

"Wow. I must have the mind of Einstein.
I can understand all this data."

B.G. Webb

"I'm Black and Beautiful. Anyone here have a problem with that?"

"I'm the reincarnation of Henny Youngman."

B.G. WEBB

"Ah -- such a macho man. I would love to have him make love to me. Well, at least I can dream about having love games with him."

"I wish I looked more like Edward R. Murrow."

"I'm not a gigolo! I'm an escort for ladies who need one."

CONCLUDING THOUGHTS ABOUT OUR JOURNEY INTO THE DREAMS, WISHES AND FANTASIES OF COMMON FOLK

Why is it so difficult for folk to reach the stars and find happiness? Why do so many get lost in the clouds along the way?

I feel that the photos, poems and sketches answered those questions. Here are the reasons:
1. not being protected, loved and appreciated as a child
2. living in a culture that judges one on material things and physical appearance
3. a fear of something or someone as a result of some trauma or the loss of something dear
4. not being included -- being treated as an outsider
5. opposing forces within a relationship -- in a marriage, family, ethnic or racial groups
6. differences between various cultural groups in terms of behaviors and outlooks.
7. being born with an ego that needs to be treated special,

Are there any solutions to help more people reach the stars and find happiness without getting side tracked and lost in the clouds?

I think there are. Naturally, we need to provide more mental health professional to help treat people.

Trained counselors in every school is a must to help young people deal with emotional problems.

Ethics should be added to the curriculum. Teachers would teach the ethics of humanitarianism. In my opinion this is essential. As humans we need to judge people as individuals and not by what they have materially and how they look.

Also, the United Nations must become more effective in dealing with cultural and political difference -- dealing with revolutions, wars, social unrest.

As citizens of this planet, we must not allow F.D.R.s dream of an effective world organization to be just a fantasy.

The same goes for the Universal Declaration of Human Rights. It is still a dream that must become a reality.

In conclusion, dreaming, wishing and fantasizing are normal forms of mental behaviors -- really safety valves to help mankind cope with the downs of life.

In some cases they give comfort and joy to us. In others they allow people to vent their fears and anger in less harmful ways.

Without these mental outlets, there would be more suicides and aggressive, indeed, criminal actions. So, we must be glad that in our evolution we developed the ability to dream, wish and fantasize.

A PERSONAL NOTE

I was the boy in the folk poem entitled, "The boy who dreamed of flaming torches and breaking glass."

In my case the brain was trying to cope with a horrible event.

I was helped through the care of mental health professionals over a number of years.

The solution came in helping me find out the truth behind my nightmares.

The truth was that I had witnessed the killing of my immediate family by Nazis in 1938 during Kristallnacht -- the Night of the Broken Glass.

The couple who raised me were not my real parents but they had kept that secret from me to protect my new identity and to prevent the authorities from taking legal action against them. You see, they were part of the underground group dedicated to saving Jews during the 1930s.

Yes, I was a child of the Night of the Broken Glass -- one of the lucky ones to escape. But, my mind retained the images of burning torches, the sound of breaking glass and the sight of blood dripping down broken window panes.

I will never know the whole story--who saved me -- who were my real parents, how and why I was given to the people who raised me, how I got to the U.S.A.

I can only wish I knew, dream about what may have happened and fantasize about the events that took place on and after that horrible night.

B.G. WEBB

ABOUT THE AUTHOR

"So, when I blow out the candles, what should I wish for?"

B.G. Webb was born in Moline, Illinois. He earned a B.A. from Augustana College and later a M.A. in history at the U. of Illinois.

He taught social studies for thirty-three years, mainly at Webster Groves High School in St. Louis County.

During his years as a teacher, he wrote five articles that were published in professional journals about some of his creative courses and teaching methods.

He did a lot of team teaching with staff members from the English, Drama and Art Departments. They developed such courses as Humanities and International Relations.

This experience helps explain his writing efforts –– all approached from a multi-arts point of view. He combines photos and art along with poetry to develop a theme.

His use of what he calls "folk poetry" may be new. He writes his poems about the common folk and does it in a way that places stress not on rhyming or meter but telling a story in such a way as to develop the emotional aspects of the tale. If rhyming and meter fit in, he uses them.

In 2016 Author House published his work entitled, Echoes and Shadows of Life: As Revealed in Folk Poetry, Old Photographs and Art. In the same year Author House published his Nights of the Black Moon and Days of Sunshine Among Common Folk.

His earlier works are: Home Front Diary –– 1944, Voices and Shadows of Old Moline, and Up Close and Very Personal.

Printed in the United States
by Bookmasters

Printed in the United States
By Bookmasters